Patrick Chan

by Jennifer Sutoski

CAPSTONE PRESS
a capstone imprint

Pebble Plus is published by Capstone Press,
1710 Roe Crest Drive, North Mankato, Minnesota 56003
www.capstonepub.com

Library of Congress Cataloging-in-Publication Data
Cataloging-in-publication information is on file with the Library of Congress.

ISBN 978–1-4914-7834-9 (library binding : alk. paper)
ISBN 978–1-4914-7842-4 (pbk. : alk. paper)
ISBN 978–1-4914-7857-8 (eBook PDF)

Developed and Produced by Discovery Books Limited
Paul Humphrey: project manager
Sabrina Crewe: editor
Ian Winton: designer

Photo Credits
Iurii Osadchi/Shutterstock: cover, 19 (main image); Olga Besnard/Shutterstock: title page, 17 (bottom left); Igor Demchenkov/Shutterstock: 5 (main image); Carlos Osorio/Toronto Star/Getty Images: 5 (inset); Elena Elisseeva/Shutterstock: 7 (main image); Skate Canada Archives/©Skate Canada: 7 (inset); Wikimedia Commons: 9; Reuters/Chris Wattie/Corbis: 11; David Cooper/Toronto Star/Getty Images: 13; Alex Aranda/Shutterstock: 15 (main image); Reuters/Mike Cassese/Corbis: 15 (inset); ID1974/Shutterstock: 17 (top left); Gertan/Shutterstock: 17 (right); ©Skate Canada: 19 (inset); REUTERS/David Gray/Corbis: 21.

Note to Parents and Teachers

The Canadian Biographies set supports national curriculum standards for social studies related to people and culture. This book describes and illustrates Patrick Chan. The images support early readers in understanding text. The repetition of words and phrases helps early readers learn new words. This book also introduces early readers to subject-specific vocabulary words, which are defined in the Glossary section. Early readers may need assistance to read some words and to use the Table of Contents, Glossary, Read More, Internet Sites, and Index sections of the book.

Printed in China through World Print Ltd in 2015
007326WPF15

Table of Contents

Early Life

Patrick Lewis Wai-Kuan Chan is a famous Canadian figure skater. He was born December 31, 1990, in Ottawa, Ontario. Both his parents came to Canada from Hong Kong, China.

born in Ottawa, Ontario

1990

Patrick with his father, Lewis Chan

Hong Kong, where Patrick's parents were born

Patrick was raised in Toronto.

He started skating at age 5.

When Patrick was 10, he won

his first national medal.

Patrick's coach believed he

would be a great skater.

born in Ottawa,
Ontario

1990

2001

wins first
national medal

Osborne Colson was Patrick's first coach and mentor.

Skating in Toronto

7

A Rising Star

Patrick worked hard at school. He spoke French, English, and Chinese. Patrick also won many junior skating competitions in Canada. In 2005, he went to the Junior World Championships. He was only 14!

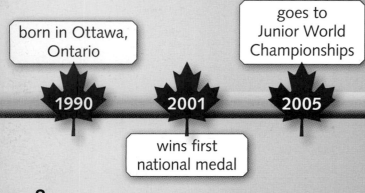

born in Ottawa, Ontario

1990

goes to Junior World Championships

2005

2001

wins first national medal

Patrick went to this high school in Toronto.

Patrick began to enter adult competitions. In 2008, he won the Canadian Figure Skating Championships. Patrick was 17 and still in school, but he was Canada's skating champion.

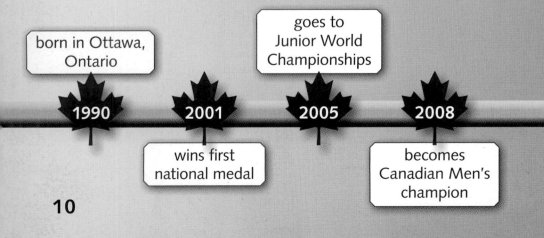

born in Ottawa, Ontario

1990

wins first national medal

2001

goes to Junior World Championships

2005

2008

becomes Canadian Men's champion

Patrick Chan competes in 2008.

Also in 2008, Patrick started

working with young athletes. He

taught kids about fitness. He talked

to them about setting goals. Patrick

had his own studies, too. He

graduated from high school in 2009.

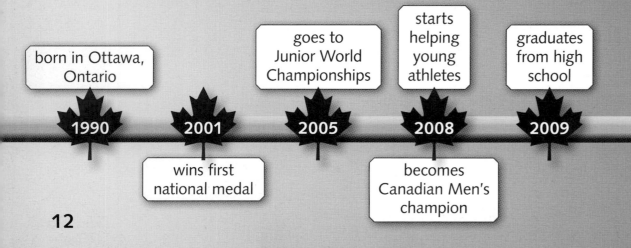

born in Ottawa,
Ontario

goes to
Junior World
Championships

starts
helping
young
athletes

graduates
from high
school

1990   2001   2005   2008   2009

wins first
national medal

becomes
Canadian Men's
champion

Patrick visits a kids' skating program.

In 2010, Patrick skated at his first Olympic Games, in Vancouver. Patrick said skating in the Olympics made him proud to be Canadian. He didn't win, but he decided to try harder.

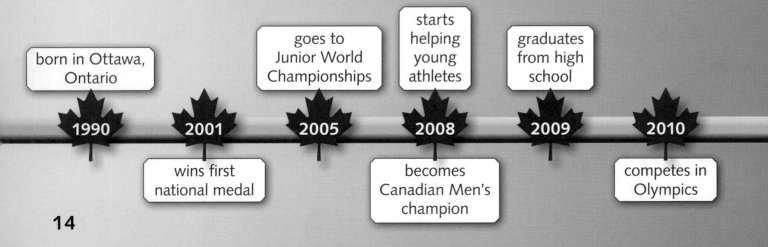

born in Ottawa, Ontario

1990

wins first national medal

2001

goes to Junior World Championships

2005

starts helping young athletes

2008

becomes Canadian Men's champion

graduates from high school

2009

2010

competes in Olympics

Patrick at practice in 2010 after the Olympics

Patrick skates at the 2010 Olympic Games.

World Champion

In 2011, Patrick went to Moscow, Russia. There, he won the World Championships. He skated so well that he set three world records. Patrick kept winning in 2012 and 2013.

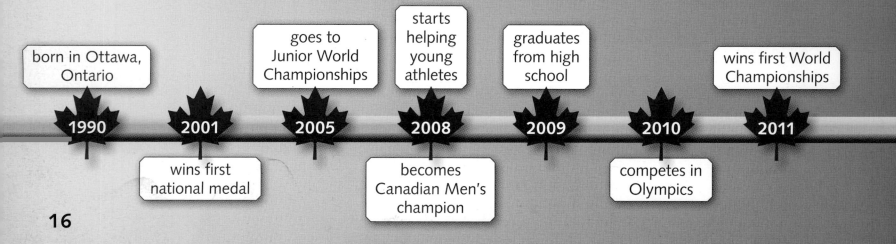

born in Ottawa, Ontario — 1990

wins first national medal — 2001

goes to Junior World Championships — 2005

starts helping young athletes — 2008

becomes Canadian Men's champion — 2008

graduates from high school — 2009

competes in Olympics — 2010

wins first World Championships — 2011

Patrick wins the World Championships again in 2012.

Winning another trophy in 2011

In 2014, it was time for the Olympic Games again. This time, the Olympics were in Russia. Patrick won two silver medals for Canada.

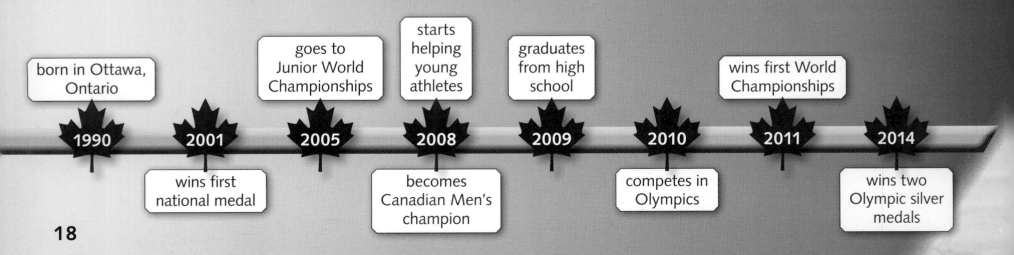

born in Ottawa, Ontario

1990

wins first national medal

2001

goes to Junior World Championships

2005

starts helping young athletes

2008

becomes Canadian Men's champion

graduates from high school

2009

competes in Olympics

2010

wins first World Championships

2011

2014

wins two Olympic silver medals

Patrick won two medals at the 2014 Olympics.

19

More to Come

After the Olympics, Patrick took a break from winning medals. He focused on his training. Patrick enjoys other sports, such as tennis and skiing. He still finds time to help young athletes.

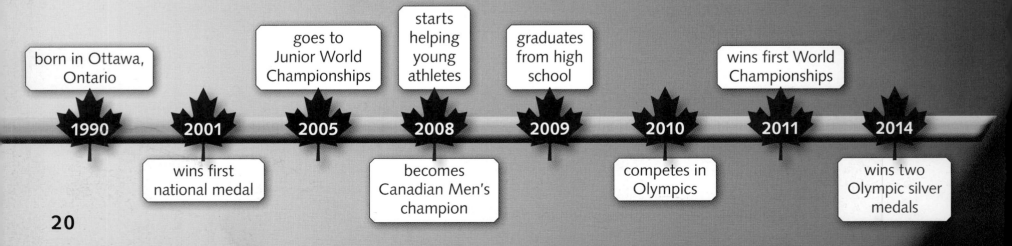

born in Ottawa, Ontario

goes to Junior World Championships

starts helping young athletes

graduates from high school

wins first World Championships

1990 **2001** **2005** **2008** **2009** **2010** **2011** **2014**

wins first national medal

becomes Canadian Men's champion

competes in Olympics

wins two Olympic silver medals

Patrick works hard with his coach, Kathy Johnson.

Glossary

athlete—a person who is good at one or several sports

championships—the games or contests that decide who is
   the best of all

coach—a person who trains an athlete

figure skater—a person who skates patterns on ice

focus—to place all attention on one thing

goal—something a person aims to reach or do

mentor—a person to look up to and learn from

national—to do with the whole country

Olympic Games—world event at which countries compete in
   many different sports

training—practising over and over to do something until you
   are ready

world record—the best in the world

Read More

Browning, Kurt. *A is for Axel: An Ice Skating Alphabet.* North Mankato, MN: Cherry Lake Publishing, 2005.

Throp, Claire. *Figure Skating.* Chicago, IL: Raintree, 2013.

Internet Sites

FactHound offers a safe, fun way to find Internet sites related to this book. All of the sites on FactHound have been researched by our staff.

Here's all you do:

Visit *www.facthound.com*

Type in this code: 9781491478349

Super-cool stuff! Check out projects, games and lots more at **www.capstonekids.com**

Index